FRANCIS FRITH'S

AROUND RICHMOND

PHOTOGRAPHIC MEMORIES

JANE HATCHER is an architectural and local historian. She lives in Richmond, but her interest in architecture and history stems from her childhood in York. A well-known author, lecturer and researcher, she has made radio broadcasts and television appearances, and one of her recent research commissions was a report for the North-East Civic Trust on Gayle Mill, a building in Wensleydale which featured in the second series of the BBC's 'Restoration' programme in 2004. She has recently been working as Local Studies Co-ordinator for Durham County Council. Her hobbies include growing her own vegetables.

FRANCIS FRITH'S
PHOTOGRAPHIC MEMORIES

AROUND RICHMOND

PHOTOGRAPHIC MEMORIES

JANE HATCHER

First published in the United Kingdom in 2004 by
Frith Book Company Ltd

Limited Hardback Subscribers Edition Published in 2004
ISBN 1-85937-839-0

Paperback Edition 2004
ISBN 1-85937-383-6

British Library Cataloguing in Publication Data

Francis Frith's Around Richmond - Photographic Memories
Jane Hatcher

Frith Book Company Ltd
Frith's Barn, Teffont,
Salisbury, Wiltshire SP3 5QP
Tel: +44 (0) 1722 716 376
Email: info@francisfrith.co.uk
www.francisfrith.co.uk

Printed and bound in Great Britain

Front Cover: **RICHMOND**, *The Castle Keep 1908* 59493
Frontispiece: **MARKET PLACE**, *c1965* R32090

*The colour-tinting is for illustrative purposes only, and is not intended
to be historically accurate*

AS WITH ANY HISTORICAL DATABASE THE FRITH ARCHIVE IS
CONSTANTLY BEING CORRECTED AND IMPROVED AND THE
PUBLISHERS WOULD WELCOME INFORMATION ON OMISSIONS OR
INACCURACIES

CONTENTS

FRANCIS FRITH: VICTORIAN PIONEER   *7*

RICHMOND - AN INTRODUCTION   *10*

RICHMOND - THE MARKET PLACE   *15*

RICHMOND - THE CASTLE AND THE RIVER SWALE   *28*

MORE OF RICHMOND   *44*

RICHMOND ENVIRONS   *66*

INDEX   *89*

NAMES OF SUBSCRIBERS   *90*

Free Mounted Print Voucher   *93*

FRANCIS FRITH
VICTORIAN PIONEER

FRANCIS FRITH, founder of the world-famous photographic archive, was a complex and multi-talented man. A devout Quaker and a highly successful Victorian businessman, he was philosophical by nature and pioneering in outlook.

By 1855 he had already established a wholesale grocery business in Liverpool, and sold it for the astonishing sum of £200,000, which is the equivalent today of over £15,000,000. Now a very rich man, he was able to indulge his passion for travel. As a child he had pored over travel books written by early explorers, and his fancy and imagination had been stirred by family holidays to the sublime mountain regions of Wales and Scotland. 'What lands of spirit-stirring and enriching scenes and places!' he had written. He was to return to these scenes of grandeur in later years to 'recapture the thousands of vivid and tender memories', but with a different purpose. Now in his thirties, and captivated by the new science of photography, Frith set out on a series of pioneering journeys up the Nile and to the Near East that occupied him from 1856 until 1860.

INTRIGUE AND EXPLORATION

These far-flung journeys were packed with intrigue and adventure. In his life story, written when he was sixty-three, Frith tells of being held captive by bandits, and of fighting 'an awful midnight battle to the very point of surrender with a deadly pack of hungry, wild dogs'. Wearing flowing Arab costume, Frith arrived at Akaba by camel sixty years before Lawrence of Arabia, where he encountered 'desert princes and rival sheikhs, blazing with jewel-hilted swords'.

He was the first photographer to venture beyond the sixth cataract of the Nile. Africa was still the mysterious 'Dark Continent', and Stanley and Livingstone's historic meeting was a decade into the future. The conditions for picture taking confound belief. He laboured for hours in his wicker dark-room in the sweltering heat of the desert, while the volatile chemicals fizzed dangerously in their trays. Back in London he exhibited his photographs and was 'rapturously cheered' by members of the Royal Society. His reputation as a photographer was made overnight.

VENTURE OF A LIFE-TIME

Characteristically, Frith quickly spotted the opportunity to create a new business as a specialist publisher of photographs. He lived in an era of immense and sometimes violent change.

For the poor in the early part of Victoria's reign work was exhausting and the hours long, and people had precious little free time to enjoy themselves. Most had no transport other than a cart or gig at their disposal, and rarely travelled far beyond the boundaries of their own town or village. However, by the 1870s the railways had threaded their way across the country, and Bank Holidays and half-day Saturdays had been made obligatory by Act of Parliament. All of a sudden the working man and his family were able to enjoy days out and see a little more of the world.

With typical business acumen, Francis Frith foresaw that these new tourists would enjoy having souvenirs to commemorate their days out. In 1860 he married Mary Ann Rosling and set out on a new career: his aim was to photograph every city, town and village in Britain. For the next thirty years he travelled the country by train and by pony and trap, producing fine photographs of seaside resorts and beauty spots that were keenly bought by millions of Victorians. These prints were painstakingly pasted into family albums and pored over during the dark nights of winter, rekindling precious memories of summer excursions.

THE RISE OF FRITH & CO

Frith's studio was soon supplying retail shops all over the country. To meet the demand he gathered about him a small team of photographers, and published the work of independent artist-photographers of the calibre of Roger Fenton and Francis Bedford. In order to gain some understanding of the scale of Frith's business one only has to look at the catalogue issued by Frith & Co in 1886: it runs to some 670 pages, listing not only many thousands of views of the British Isles but also many photographs of most European countries, and China, Japan, the USA and Canada - note the sample page shown on page 9 from the hand-written Frith & Co ledgers recording the pictures. By 1890 Frith had created the greatest specialist photographic publishing company in the world, with over 2,000 sales outlets - more than the combined number that Boots and WH Smith have today! The picture on the next page shows the Frith & Co display board at Ingleton in the Yorkshire Dales (left of window). Beautifully constructed with a mahogany frame and gilt inserts, it could display up to a dozen local scenes.

POSTCARD BONANZA

The ever-popular holiday postcard we know today took many years to develop. In 1870 the Post Office issued the first plain cards, with a pre-printed stamp on one face. In 1894 they allowed other publishers' cards to be sent through the mail with an attached adhesive halfpenny stamp. Demand grew rapidly, and in 1895 a new size of postcard was permitted called the court card, but there was little room for illustration. In 1899, a year after Frith's death, a new card measuring 5.5 x 3.5 inches became the standard format, but it was not until 1902 that the divided back came into being, so that the address and message could be on one face and a full-size illustration on the other. Frith & Co were in the vanguard of postcard development: Frith's sons Eustace and Cyril continued their father's monumental task, expanding the number of views offered to the public and recording more and more places in Britain, as the coasts and countryside were opened up to mass travel.

Francis Frith had died in 1898 at his villa in Cannes, his great project still growing. The archive he created continued in business for another seventy years. By 1970 it contained over a third of a million pictures showing 7,000 British towns and villages.

FRANCIS FRITH'S LEGACY

Frith's legacy to us today is of immense significance and value, for the magnificent archive of evocative photographs he created provides a unique record of change in the cities, towns and villages throughout Britain over a century and more. Frith and his fellow studio photographers revisited locations many times down the years to update their views, compiling for us an enthralling and colourful pageant of British life and character.

We are fortunate that Frith was dedicated to recording the minutiae of everyday life. For it is this sheer wealth of visual data, the painstaking chronicle of changes in dress, transport, street layouts, buildings, housing, engineering and landscape that captivates us so much today. His remarkable images offer us a powerful link with the past and with the lives of our ancestors.

THE VALUE OF THE ARCHIVE TODAY

Computers have now made it possible for Frith's many thousands of images to be accessed almost instantly. Frith's images are increasingly used as visual resources, by social historians, by researchers into genealogy and ancestry, by architects and town planners, and by teachers involved in local history projects.

In addition, the archive offers every one of us an opportunity to examine the places where we and our families have lived and worked down the years. Highly successful in Frith's own era, the archive is now, a century and more on, entering a new phase of popularity. Historians consider the Francis Frith Collection to be of prime national importance. It is the only archive of its kind remaining in private ownership. Francis Frith's archive is now housed in an historic timber barn in the beautiful village of Teffont in Wiltshire. Its founder would not recognize the archive office as it is today. In place of the many thousands of dusty boxes containing glass plate negatives and an all-pervading odour of photographic chemicals, there are now ranks of computer screens. He would be amazed to watch his images travelling round the world at unimaginable speeds through internet lines.

The archive's future is both bright and exciting. Francis Frith, with his unshakeable belief in making photographs available to the greatest number of people, would undoubtedly approve of what is being done today with his lifetime's work. His photographs depicting our shared past are now bringing pleasure and enlightenment to millions around the world a century and more after his death.

RICHMOND
AN INTRODUCTION

IN 2002 RICHMOND was voted by readers of 'Country Life' magazine eighth among the ten best places to live, judged on character, heritage and public amenities. To modern eyes the town seems a quaint little backwater, still beautiful owing to its setting, its townscape and old buildings relatively unspoiled, a place where traditions linger. Richmond was historically a place of significance, and this writer regrets that its importance continues to be eroded in the early 21st century. The Frith archive amply illustrates Richmond's townscape and geographical setting, both changed and unchanged, over the period 1892 to c1965.

Richmond is the market town for Swaledale, one of the beautiful V-shaped valleys forming the Yorkshire Dales. One might think that Richmond is situated on the steep north bank of the River Swale because its south-facing aspect made it a good place to establish a town. In fact, the spot is not ideal, owing to its hills and lack of drinking water. Rather, Richmond owes its origins to its spectacularly defensive site high above the River Swale. This commended it to Count Alan Rufus of Brittany, kinsman of William the Conqueror, who about the year 1071

built the castle as the prestigious headquarters of an immense area of feudal land-holdings later known as the Honour of Richmond. Most early Norman castles were motte-and-bailey earthworks, but Richmond was one of the first stone-built castles in the country. In addition to the triangular Great Court, there was a smaller east court, the Cockpit, and a large outer bailey, now the present Market Place. The magnificent keep, almost 100ft tall, which was added by Conan, Duke of Brittany in the second half of the 12th century, is a superb example of Norman military architecture.

Despite the defensive quality of the site, there is no indication of earlier settlement here. Roman coins have been found, but no evidence of Roman occupation, although Quaker Lane follows the line of a Roman road leading to lead mines in Swaledale. Most surrounding villages are of older origin than Richmond. The town's eastern boundary is a much older earthwork called Scots Dike. In the Dark Ages this was the eastern defence of Rheged, a British kingdom which sought to protect itself against neighbouring Anglian kingdoms of Deira and Bernicia. Richmond thus also marks a strategic junction of two different ancient cultural traditions, with significant differences of topography, agriculture, place-names and even dialect above and below the town. On the south side, Richmond's boundary is the middle of the River Swale, and on the seven-yearly Boundary Riding the mayor has to be carried into the middle of the river!

Richmond is the 'mother' of the fifty-plus Richmonds throughout the world, and claims that there are more of this place-name than any other. The first 'daughter' Richmond was Sheen in Surrey; its palace was rebuilt after a fire and re-named in 1499 by Henry VII, one of whose titles was Earl of Richmond (Yorkshire). The name is from the 'riche mont' or 'fine and noble hill' of the Norman-French settlers.

The town which grew up around the castle was soon granted certain privileges of self government, including the weekly Saturday market which is still an important part of Richmond life. The Norman town was split between two suburbs, Newbiggin, probably the original market place, and Frenchgate, with the parish church; another developed along Bargate, leading to the river crossing and The Green, an industrial area near the River Swale. The word Swale comes from the Old English 'suala', meaning swirling and rushing (as in the bird swallow). The river was not only a boundary and barrier, it also powered a number of watermills, initially for grinding corn, then for fulling, and later for paper-making and even some textile spinning.

Medieval Richmond increased in size and status: subsequent charters granted three annual fairs. The strip system of agriculture was practised on three great open fields - West Field, Gallow Field to the north, and East Field. Today only the first, now known as Westfields, remains substantially open.

Castle Walk 1893 32277

When Scottish raids were a nuisance in the early 14th century, the townsfolk moved into the Outer Bailey, and obtained permission to defend it with the Town Wall, which was built in about 1311. The Market Place, still referred to as the Bailey into the 19th century, is therefore of unusual size, horse-shoe shaped and sloping. The Town Wall necessarily had few openings: there were two for vehicular access in Finkle Street and the Channel, and two surviving pedestrian posterns in Friars Wynd and Cornforth Hill. The gateways are called bars in northern dialect. Much of the dialect, place-names and street names have their origins in Scandinavian languages; an example is the word 'wynd', pronounced to rhyme with win, which means a narrow lane leading through, and not a dead-end. These few openings in the Town Wall limited traffic movement until New Road was formed in 1774 and King Street in 1813.

Trinity Church is a relic of the Outer Bailey. Its tower belongs to the town, not the church; it houses the town clock, and the bells, which ring not only the time but the Apprentice Bell each morning, the Curfew Bell each evening, and on Shrove Tuesday the Pancake Bell. Each September there is a First Fruits ceremony, when the first local farmer to complete his harvest presents a 'goodly sample' of it to the Mayor.

The Tudor period saw considerable changes. The castle, declining in importance for some time, was finally allowed to fall into disrepair. The reign of Henry VIII saw the Dissolution of the religious houses which had been established nearby - such as the Greyfriars, Easby Abbey, and St Martin's Priory, a disaster which must have profoundly affected the town's economic prosperity and social infrastructure. Indeed,

Richmond played a major part in the Pilgrimage of Grace, a rebellion against the Dissolution. At the end of the 16th century a plague caused the deaths of over a thousand people, perhaps half the town's population. An unusual personal link with the Tudor dynasty is a rare contemporary portrait of Queen Elizabeth I, which hangs in the Town Council Chamber.

No Civil War skirmishes were fought nearby, but Prince Rupert attempted to rally his defeated army here after the Battle of Marston Moor in 1644. The Scottish army, occupying the area for the victorious Parliamentarians, was based on St Nicholas, an ancient house on the outskirts of the town, and the soldiers not only caused considerable damage, but brought another outbreak of the plague.

Richmond's heyday was in Georgian times. Its beauty and medieval ruins gave it the picturesque qualities then newly fashionable, and it became a leading provincial centre for social activities, with race meetings, assemblies, balls, musters of the North York Militia - and plays in the miraculously surviving Georgian Theatre Royal. Richmond was particularly known as a respectable but modest place for comfortably-off widows to retire to. Promenades were created where people could go to 'see and to be seen' among those of social consequence, and so we have the Castle Walk and the Terrace, both of which feature in the Frith photographs, and also walks in Billy Banks Wood and Easby Woods. Not only were Georgian town houses built, mainly in local stone but occasionally in brick, but also elegant gardens were created. Owing to the more transient nature of gardens they have left less surviving evidence than the architecture, but a folly, Culloden Tower, is prominent in many views of the town. It is surprising that it hardly appears in the Frith postcards.

Georgian prosperity saw much of the town's infrastructure improved - new roads were built both within the town and leading out from it as turnpike roads, the bridge was rebuilt, and a new toll booth was built in the Market Place as a base for trade regulation. Demolished in 1948, it can be seen in many photographs. The medieval market cross was replaced by the obelisk, inscribed 'Rebuilt AD1771, Christopher Wayne, Esq, Mayor'. Its stepped plinth concealed a reservoir to improve the supply of drinking water. The town's medieval Grammar School, re-founded by Queen Elizabeth I, came to outstanding prominence under the Mastership of James Tate, son of a local maltster, born in Bank Yard just off the Market Place.

Richmond became the terminus of a branch railway line from Darlington built by the 'Railway King' George Hudson. It opened in 1846, and all the buildings along the line were designed in a 'Tudorbethan' style by York architect George Townsend Andrews. The passenger station had iron columns cast by John Walker, the York ironfounder who made the British Museum railings. That Richmond had such an elegant and relatively early railway says much about the importance of the town. Although starting to decline (it was hoped the railway would reverse that), it was still a place where a line was considered viable. As well as providing outbound transport for local lead and wool, the railway met the demand for County Durham coal from a population much expanded during Georgian times. The railway had an additional effect in introducing Welsh roofing slates to augment the traditional stone slates and clay pantiles.

The railway also brought visitors - who bought postcards! Thomas Spencer, a Market Place stationer who printed postcards, almanacs and booklets on local history, did much to popularise local legends such as the Lass of

Queens Road 1898 41643

Richmond Hill, Robert Willance, Potter Thompson and the Little Drummer Boy. This last alludes to the town's on-going military associations, from the North York Militia, through the Green Howards to Catterick Camp. Begun in 1915, and re-named Catterick Garrison in 1973, this is now the largest military base in Europe, and an important part of Richmond's economy. The number of troops based here increased dramatically during both World Wars, and many men still associate Richmond with their time as National Servicemen. From the 1920s war memorials appear in the photographs, which also show iron railings sacrificed during the Second World War.

What the Frith views omit is interesting. We see an operative cinema, but only a closed Georgian Theatre, and there is no hint of the important racehorse-training tradition. Several of the pictures were taken in 1929, a year which saw the commemoration of the sixth centenary of the Richmond charter granted in 1329 by King Edward III, but none of this pageantry is shown. Indeed, there is nothing of the civic ceremony which is an important part of Richmond life, despite the loss of borough status in 1974.

Some photographs show areas open where now there is housing, but the decline in Richmond as a shopping centre is particularly evident. Not only are there far fewer drapers, grocers and butchers, but the shopping area has contracted to an area barely extending beyond the Market Place. Frith shows shops in Frenchgate, Castle Hill and New Road. A similar trend is reflected in the pictures of villages, taken because there were once village shops and post offices which were points of sale.

WILLANCE'S LEAP, *The Monuments and the Caravan Site c1965* R32080

RICHMOND – THE MARKET PLACE

RICHMOND'S cobbled Market Place is the town's focus. Its size and shape stem from its origin as the outer bailey of Richmond Castle. It was encompassed by the medieval Town Wall, which restricted access to it until Georgian improvements saw the formation of new roads. In the centre of the Market Place stand the market obelisk and Trinity Church. Some older photographs show now-demolished buildings, such as parts of Trinity Church Square, and the Toll Booth, a large Georgian building once at the centre of the town's commercial life.

The Frith photographs inevitably document the transition from carts to cars, the changing styles and numbers of both cars and buses parked in the Market Place, and older shop fronts. A more subtle change recorded is that from family-owned businesses to chain stores, and the gradual reduction in the number of drapers and food retailers operating in the Market Place.

Market Place c1965 R32090

This relatively recent view at first seems little changed from today, but none of the shops now bear the same name, and only three sell the same wares. Most shops here are family run, but Timothy White's (later Boots - centrally between the obelisk and Trinity Church) and Burton's (right of Trinity Tower) suggest changes to come. On King Street corner is Clarkson the chemist, whose shop interior went to Preston Park museum on Teesside. The obelisk has cars parked around its stepped base, but now there are more, and closer to it. Trinity Church has not yet become the Green Howards' Regimental Headquarters and Museum, and beyond Greyfriars Tower is the Grammar School Cricket Field, to become the Co-op Superstore in 1998.

Market Place
c1908 59492

This is a conspicuously older view. It is Saturday afternoon, just after 2.00pm. Trade is quiet; one hopes the large stall well-stocked with boots and shoes has done better business earlier. Goods are being packed up into large wicker hampers, and perhaps some stallholders have already repaired to one of the town's many inns - 'market fresh' was a local expression for having had rather too much to drink.

▶ *Market Place 1929*
82551

Percival's Swaledale Motor Services run buses (left) between Richmond and the Swaledale villages. The few people with motor cars park them at will. The ball finial of the Obelisk looks new; it had been replaced in 1907. At least one household living upstairs in the Toll Booth has lit a fire. The Bishop Blaize Hotel (right) commemorates the patron saint of wool combers, sore throats and cowherds!

◀ *Market Place 1893* 32280

Perhaps it is the time of one of the annual fairs, rather than an ordinary market day, as stalls can be seen on both sides of Trinity Church Square. The vehicles which the traders have used to bring their wares can be seen in the foreground; often these were parked outside the Market Place in Queens Road. The horses and ponies which pulled the carts were stabled behind the town's many inns, where they were fed, watered and rested, ready for the journey home. Some of those coming into the town may have had their hair cut by Charles Todd, the hairdresser whose premises can be seen at the extreme right of the building to the right of Trinity Tower.

▲ *Market Place 1923* 74351

Most of these shops had a long history. Spencer's the stationer's beyond Finkle Street sold postcards, perhaps including Frith's! Next is Haywood's, which until 1984 always displayed horse-racing memorabilia alongside the shoes in its window. Wallace's and Hodgson's were drapers, Whitell was a grocer, and Robert Spence an ironmonger. Only Tennet the grocer's, second from left, has continued, with several name changes; it is currently Ken Warne's.

◄ *Trinity Church c1965* R32070

On this sunny early afternoon Di Palma Cream Ices and Johnny's Creamy Ices compete for trade (centre), and people sit in the rose garden formed next to Trinity Church after the iron railings, visible in 82553 (pages 21-22), were sent for salvage during the Second World War. The No 25 Scorton bus waits in its bay; in those days metal barriers guided the bus queues.

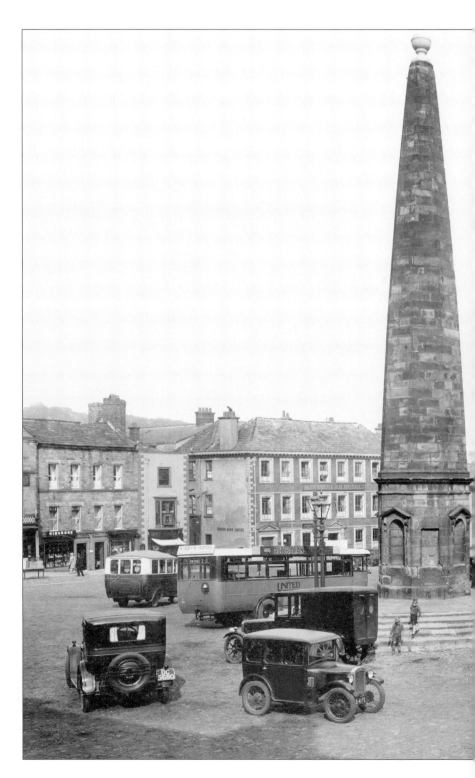

Market Place
1929 82553

The restoration of
Trinity Tower has just
been completed after the
demolition of some
of the buildings in
Trinity Church Square
in 1923 – compare this
photograph with picture
74351 (page 19). On the
right is part of the Toll
Booth. United have joined
Percival's in providing local
bus services.

▼ *Trinity Church and the Castle 1913* 65476

Outside King & Son (centre right) can be seen their saddle-horse, and beyond is the barber's pole of W Myers, who succeeded hairdresser Charles Todd, visible in 32280 (page 18). Both these buildings were demolished in 1923. Hiding much of the castle keep is the Toll Booth.

▶ *Trinity Church 1913* 65475

Shops were created below the north aisle of Trinity Church when it was restored in 1864. Previously the north aisle had housed the Consistory Court of the Archdeaconry of Richmond. Four antique chairs outside the shop of G Parmley & Sons (left) doubtless contrasted in price with the cheap presents and postcards of H Blow's Bazaar next door. Next to the church entrance is the shop of T J Lodge, one of the town's nine butchers in 1913, with a similar number attending the weekly market. The billboards displayed beside the doorway leading into Trinity Tower advertise property auctions and Darlington sports. Above is mounted the chain which rang the town's fire alarm, a bell in the tower.

◄ *Market Place 1929*
82555

Railings mark where King's shop had stood. The butcher's has become a shop selling paintings and engravings, the Bazaar is now Lucy Wilcox's cigarettes and sweets shop, but Parmley's Antiques is still in business. On the left is part of Bainbridge & Co's shop window – they were drapers and tailors.

► *Market Place 1929*
82550

On the left outside Rodber's furniture and floor coverings shop can be seen tables, beds and a chest of drawers, and also their delivery van. Cookes next door was a printer and stationer selling postcards, and then came A G Metcalfe, a baker with café, and R S Corner, a confectioner. Beyond, the grocer between the banks was now Singleton's. On the right, in front of the Toll Booth gable-end, is a weighbridge.

▶ *Market Place from the Castle Keep c1955*
R32013

The amount of change since 1929 is surprisingly small, although Cookes the stationer's has become Austin's. Below the second window of the building marked 'Restaurant' (the fifth building from the left) is the opening to Bank Yard, named after the Old Bank which occupied the building in 1792. The roofs behind, parallel to the High Row of the Market Place, are houses in Waterloo Street, demolished in 1963.

◀ *Market Place c1965*
R32068

The increased number of cars is suddenly very noticeable, and parking bays have been painted on the cobbles. The long-established but name-changing grocer's between the Midland and National Provincial Banks has changed from Singleton's to Relton's (third from the left), and would become Jopling's before becoming Ken Warnes. Timothy Whites the chemist (right) will soon become Boots.

▲ *The King's Head Hotel 1913* 65481

Built as a town house for the lead mine-owner Charles Bathurst of Arkengarthdale c1720, its newly-fashionable hand-made bricks, three-storey height and eight bays must then have made it very prominent in the Market Place. It was converted into the King's Head almost immediately, and remains the town's largest hotel. The doorway on the extreme right served as the bar entrance, and another doorway was inserted to the left when Lloyds Bank opened here c1920. King Street on the left was so named not from this hotel but from the King's Arms Inn which stood on the site until 1813, when it was demolished to make way for a more level access for carriages into the Market Place at the height of Richmond's Georgian prosperity.

◄ *Market Place c1965*
R32069

The King's Head's three doorways can be seen, and the inn-signs of a carved bunch of grapes and a portrait of King Charles II. The hotel bedrooms extend over Woolworth's next door, Richmond's first chain store; it arrived c1935 and moved in 1980 to Bailey House, visible at the bottom of the Market Place. Local businesses have now been joined by Fine Fare (centre) and, extreme right, Walter Willson's.

The View from the Castle c1965 R32091

The Channel, the main access to the Market Place before the formation of King Street, is in the centre, continuing up towards the top left as Frenchgate, past St Mary's parish church. The large building to the left behind the Castle Tavern is the Methodist chapel in Ryder's Wynd, replacing an earlier chapel nearby, and superseded by the present Methodist church in Queens Road.

RICHMOND - THE CASTLE AND THE RIVER SWALE

THE SWALE, one of Richmond's most beautiful features, can be very treacherous, rising suddenly after heavy rain and sometimes causing damaging floods. Defending the promontory on which Richmond stands, it is one of the reasons why Richmond is here.

Many views of Richmond are dominated by the castle, particularly its fine 12th-century keep, which at almost 100ft tall towers above the town; its top provided Frith with a useful vantage point for several photographs. The late 11th-century triangular Great Court is surrounded by curtain walls, with Scolland's Hall in the south-east corner.

The ruined castle was a major attraction during Richmond's Georgian heyday. Its owner, the Duke of Richmond, created a fashionable promenade, Castle Walk, around it. The castle was leased to the North York Militia in 1854, and several new military buildings were erected shortly before the outbreak of the Crimean War. The castle is now in the guardianship of English Heritage, who commissioned a Contemporary Heritage Garden for the outer court known as the Cockpit.

The Castle from the South 1929
82538

This impressive view shows the whole site. Left of the keep can be seen the barracks of c1855, demolished in 1931. The first-floor room at the left-hand end with the additional bay window was the office of Lord Robert Baden-Powell, founder of the Scout and Guide Movements, when based here between 1908 and 1910 to plan a new military base, now Catterick Garrison. Castle Walk runs around the base of the castle. Below, but actually on the south side of the river, is Earl's Orchard; the flat field is now used for football, and according to tradition, it is where the knights practised their jousting. In the foreground are the cottage roofs of Sleegill.

▲ *The Castle, the Keep and Robin Hood's Tower 1913* 66022

Outside the 19th-century cell block, where Conscientious Objectors were imprisoned in 1916, stands the Sebastopol cannon, long since gone, brought to the town in 1858 and accompanied on its journey from the railway station by a procession which included excited schoolboys. To the right is Robin Hood's Tower; its ground floor contains the 11th-century St Nicholas' Chapel.

◀ *detail from 66022*

▶ *Scolland's Hall from the Castle Keep c1955* R32012

Scolland, Lord of Bedale, a knight of the castle garrison, has given his name to the 11th-century Great Hall in the south-east corner of the inner court. On the first floor, it was accessed by an external staircase just in front of the two marching figures. The Solar and the Gold Hole Tower are at the left-hand end.

◀ *The Castle, the Golden Tower 1913* 66028

Now called the Gold Hole Tower, it housed latrines serving Scolland's Hall and the battlements: perhaps those assigned the unenviable task of occasionally cleaning it out from this side were told that gold was buried here, leading to its euphemistic name! The picture is taken from the Cockpit, where English Heritage have created a Contemporary Heritage Garden designed by Neil Swanson.

▲ *Castle Walk 1893* 32278

This Georgian promenade around the base of the castle provides impressive vistas of the river below and across to the other side. Looking east, the steep bank has a low covering of bushes which obscure the views if allowed to grow up, and in 2004 a lot of clearing work was done.

◄ *Castle Walk 1893* 32277

We are looking west towards the Green Bridge, with the castle rock more visible here. The young woman on the right needs her parasol, because Castle Walk is a south-facing sun trap. A section of this part of Castle Walk has recently been fenced against the sheer drop.

▼ *Castle Walk 1929* 82546

In the distance is the Green, an industrial area with tanneries and a brewery as well as cottages. Since 1893 there have been improvements to Riverside Road leading to the Falls, and a new sewage outfall has been made from the Green into the River Swale.

▶ *The View from Castle Walk 1913* 65472

The Green Bridge was until 1846 Richmond's only river crossing. At its left end is the former Good Intent Inn, the name referring to a vein of copper mined in Billy Banks Wood beyond it. On the left is Earls Orchard, part of Sleegill, and, on the skyline is another hamlet, Mount Ararat, then with more cottages than now.

◀ *From the West 1908* 59491

Taken from Billy Banks Wood south of the Swale, this distant view shows the defensive site of Richmond Castle, and the town clinging precariously - and picturesquely - to the hillside, and also Castle Walk. In the centre is a terrace called Cornforth Hill.

▶ *The Castle and the Bridge 1893* 32275

Two children enjoy the riverside, as many still do today. The Green Bridge, named because of its proximity to the Green, was built 1788-89 to a design by the North Riding bridgemaster, York architect John Carr, after its medieval predecessor was badly damaged by a great flood in 1771.

The Castle and the Bridge 1923 74350

Children play in the River Swale when it is very low after a summer drought, but it is a very treacherous river which rises very quickly if heavy rain falls in Swaledale, and it has claimed many lives over the centuries.

▲ *The Castle and the Bridge 1892* 30654

An artist has set up an easel, steadying its legs with stones, beside a much higher river, to paint this classic view of the castle, river and bridge. The old tanneries on the Green have since been replaced by Bridge Terrace.

▶ *detail from 30654*

The Castle and the Bridge 1929 82541

The castle, still with 19th-century military block, and its ivy-covered corner tower, is reflected in the still waters of a peaceful River Swale in evening light. The tall chimney is the brewery built on the Green about 1830.

The Castle from the Green 1898 41642

The village-like triangular Green is surrounded by cottages of varied ages and sizes. The four-storey corner building is dated 1689 on its doorway. The chains and stone bollards were erected c1840; the young horse chestnut tree had been planted in 1887 to commemorate Queen Victoria's Golden Jubilee. It was replaced in 1982. Note the gas lamp.

▶ *The Falls 1913*
65534

One of the reasons why the site of Richmond was chosen was this natural waterfall; it could power a watermill to grind corn to provide flour and provender for the castle's large population. Brown trout, heading upstream each autumn to their breeding grounds in the Swale's tributaries, have to jump these falls, which in local dialect are called the Foss (or Force) Head.

◀ *The Falls c1960* R32044

This photograph shows the remains of the weir added across the top of the waterfall to increase the power to the nearby Castle Mill, which was extended by the paper maker James Cooke in 1865. A great flood destroyed the paper mill on 29 January 1883, and without maintenance the weir deteriorated. In 1972 Richmond Borough Council rebuilt half of the weir in their part of the River Swale; the rest beyond the Borough boundary was never completed. The Batts was opened up, and the riverside area was improved as a leisure attraction, which the falls already were, as we can see in this summer view.

▲ *From the River 1923* 74348

Some women artists paint the view of Richmond from across the River Swale. In the left distance can be seen smoke rising from the gasworks beside the falls. Richmond had one of the earliest gasworks in Europe, built in 1820 to provide street lighting for the fashionable Georgian town.

◄ *From the Terrace 1898*
41641

The Terrace, another Georgian promenade, offers a spectacular panorama of the town. On the right is St Mary's parish church, in the centre the Grammar School, and to the left Church Mill, demolished in 1969, the last of many Richmond watermills once powered by the River Swale.

▼ *The Railway Bridge 1892* 30660

The bridge was constructed to give road access to the railway station built on the St Martin's side of the river in 1846; it was designed in the same Gothic Revival architectural style, and the parapet pinnacles carried gaslights. Known locally as Station Bridge, it was renamed Mercury Bridge in 1975 in honour of the emblem of the 8th Signals Regiment, which has the Freedom of Richmond. The bridge was severely damaged by a major flood in 2000 and had to be rebuilt. The boy is lying on the grassy riverside bank known as the Batts.

► *The River Swale and Station Bridge c1960* R32055

In 1917 a new road from Station Bridge to Catterick Camp was built by Italian prisoners of war. Troops were major users of the railway, which closed in 1968. Behind the station are the ruins of St Martin's Priory, with Easby Abbey in the top left corner. The building in the right foreground is the former National School at the bottom of Lombards Wynd.

◀ *From the Castle c1965*
R32075

The station can just be seen to the right of Station Bridge. Along the bottom are Georgian houses in Millgate. The Channel, middle left, leads from the bottom of the Market Place up Frenchgate. Above St Mary's parish church is The Terrace.

▶ *St Mary's Church 1913* 54377

The tower was constructed about 1400 by Ralph Nevill, Earl of Westmorland. The leading Victorian architect Sir George Gilbert Scott restored the church in 1858-62, replacing flat roofs of Swaledale lead with much steeper Welsh slate roofs. Among many interesting tombstones in the large churchyard are those of two Waterloo veterans. The classical column near the porch commemorates a prominent freemason Matthew Greathead, who died aged 101 in 1871.

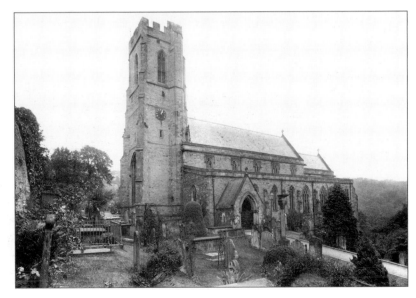

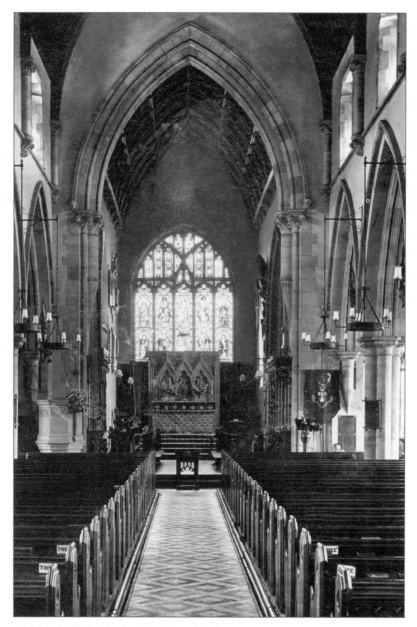

St Mary's Church, the Interior 1923 74353

The loftiness results from Scott's restoration. His are the Victorian pews, but side galleries had been removed in 1921. The regimental colours are those of the Green Howards, whose chapel is here. The Victorian reredos has been replaced by one designed as a Second World War memorial. Also in the chancel are early 16th-century choir stalls with misericords retrieved from Easby Abbey at the Dissolution.

The School c1960 R32049

Queen Elizabeth I's 1567 charter re-founding the town's medieval Grammar School housed it in the churchyard. That small school became renowned when James Tate, dubbed 'the Scholar of the North' and 'a man dripping Greek', was headmaster from 1796 to 1833. His distinguished pupils took so many Cambridge University prizes that they were called 'Tate's Invincibles'. His son and namesake succeeded him when he left to become Canon of St Paul's Cathedral. A new school was built on the riverside in 1850 in memory of the elder James, known as the Tate Testimonial. This is the central range and lower gabled wing, set between later extensions. Currently these buildings hold only the intake year of the present comprehensive Richmond School.

MORE OF RICHMOND

THE 'SUBURBS' of Frenchgate and Newbiggin, always outside the medieval walled town, both retain elegant Georgian townscapes. Bargate was the street from the Green Bridge leading to the bar, or gateway, in the town wall in Finkle Street. The medieval Greyfriars lay outside the walled town on its north side. During Richmond's period of Georgian prosperity, a number of new roads were created within that old area to improve horse-drawn traffic movements, and further improvements were made in the 19th century.

The photographic tour of the area outside the castle and the Market Place starts to the north, explores the area to the west of the walled town, and drops down almost to the riverside. From the area below the castle on its east side, the route then travels down Frenchgate. The two final locations in this section are on the eastern and western edges of the town.

From the North 1908 59489

The castle keep, Greyfriars and Trinity towers dominate the skyline. Prior House, visible through the leafless trees on the left, has been converted into apartments. Ronaldshay Park opened in 1906, and had a bandstand (right); it now has a skateboarding area. Bolton Crofts in the foreground was built on in the 1970s.

Queens Road 1898
41643

Young trees flank this extension of King Street, named to commemorate Queen Victoria's Golden Jubilee in 1887. The horse-trough survives, but semi-detached houses replaced those on the right in about 1927. The gas lamp (right) marks the corner of Quaker Lane. It must be rare for two intersecting street names to begin with a Q.

The Hospital 1913 65474

Rose Cottage (left), a handsome Gothick Revival villa on the corner of Queens Road and Quaker Lane, was extended and converted into the Victoria Cottage Hospital in 1899. Closing a century later, it is now a funeral parlour. The Victorian photographer Joseph Raine built the pair of houses on the right, set above the raised pavement which continues along Quaker Lane.

The Friary 1923
74358

The house on the left, built after the Suppression of the Greyfriars in 1539, became the headmaster's house of Richmond Grammar School in 1888. In 1898 a scholars' boarding house was added to the right. This replaced the Victoria Hospital as the Friary Community Hospital in 1999.

The Friary 1898 41648

The Friary was the Richmond town house of the Huttons, the squires of Marske; it later belonged to the Robinson family for many years. Shown just before the boarding house was added, this gentleman's residence was much enhanced by having the Greyfriars Tower (see 82556) as an interesting garden feature.

Greyfriars Tower 1929 82556

The Franciscans came to Richmond in 1258, and built a small church befitting their commitment to poverty, but this elegant belfry tower was slotted into the crossing of the church between the nave, choir and transepts in about 1500. The choir roofline can be seen on the tower, and so can the spiral staircase up to the belfry on its right. Inserting the tower on four piers inside the existing building was a great feat of engineering skill, and following the 1539 Suppression, dismantling the tower proved too difficult. Thus it survived for later generations to admire. In front is the war memorial, built after the First World War.

*Friary Gardens
c1960* R32041

This Garden of
Remembrance, opened
in 1920, is still
beautifully kept as a
memorial to sacrifices
made during both
World Wars. On the
right is a mature tree
planted in 1887. Cars
nowadays park parallel
to Queens Road.

The Fleece Hotel 1913 66031

This Scottish Baronial fantasy was designed by the Darlington architect G Gordon Hoskins in 1897. The landlord at this time, George Kinchin, offered 'First Class Family and Commercial Accommodation for Tourists', and also 'Good Stabling and Accommodation for Motors and Cycles'. He was doubtless busy for the North Yorkshire and South Durham Cyclists' Meet held each Whitsuntide. The 'Meet' is now a carnival held each Spring Bank Holiday weekend. The whitewashed wall on the corner of Friars Wynd (to the left of the hotel) is the Georgian Theatre Royal, re-opened in 1963 but in 1913 used for storage. The Friary wall on the left was set back to widen Victoria Road in 1937.

Friars Wynd 1913 65466

A fragment of the medieval Town Wall, this postern gate allowed the townsfolk to obtain drinking water from springs at the Greyfriars. The tramlines moved heavy goods between the Market Place shop of ironmonger Robert Spence and his warehouses in Friars Wynd.

King Street c1960
R32054

We are looking north towards Friary Gardens and Queens Road across the roundabout at the junction with Victoria Road. King Street became one-way for outbound traffic in 1994. Grey Friars Café (left) was built in 1889 as Cocoa Rooms by the Countess of Zetland, a staunch advocate of temperance.

▲ *King Street c1960*
R32058

The shops of the gentlemen's outfitter Cecil Halstead and the butcher C Fawcett run underneath the ballroom of the King's Head Hotel. Beyond Ryder's Wynd is the first of Richmond's two cinemas (right). Beyond is the post office, built in 1937, replacing one in Halstead's shop.

► *detail from R32058*

▲ *King Street c1955*
R32002

It was still acceptable for Brand's Garage's Shell petrol pumps to stand on the pavement (left). The cinema (beside the garage), here screening 'I'll Get By', became a bingo hall, then stood empty, and is now hardware and soft furnishings shops.

◄ *detail from R32002*

The Catholic Church 1913 65479

Richmond had a strong Roman Catholic tradition, partly due to the Lawson family of nearby Brough Hall, who gave the land here in Newbiggin for the church of St Joseph and St Francis Xavier; it was rebuilt on a larger scale in 1868. The spirelet is prominent in several vistas, a masterly touch by the architect George Goldie.

Newbiggin 1913
65465

Perhaps Richmond's most handsome and unchanged cobbled street, Newbiggin means 'new settlement'; its level width suggests that it was planned as the town's original market place. On the extreme right is the former gaol, outside which the Protestant martyr Richard Snell was burned at the stake in 1558.

Castle Hill 1929 82557

In the centre is a fish and chip saloon; to its right is the narrow wynd called The Bar, and on the railings is an advertisement for wet fish on sale in the basement of No 1 New Road. Of the shops visible here, none is still in retail use except what was Walton's pork butcher's on the Market Place corner (right). Centre left is Castle Walk.

New Road c1955 R32023

New in 1774, creating a more direct route between the Market Place and the Green Bridge, this road nevertheless has a 1 in 6 gradient. Halfway down is the shop of boot and shoe maker R McGuinness (centre). On the left, second-hand clothes have replaced fish and chips, and the railings have gone. In the distance is Culloden Tower.

The Bar 1913 65467

This is another postern gate surviving from the Town Wall, which was built to defend Richmond against Scottish raids shortly before the Battle of Bannockburn. The view looks down Cornforth Hill towards Bridge Street; the whitewashed building was the Oak Tree Inn.

The Bar 1913 65468

We are looking back in the opposite direction to 65467 through the archway towards the narrow wynd called The Bar.
The attractive houses of steeply cobbled Cornforth Hill have front gardens on the left. The house on the right, now one, was
then two.

Millgate 1913 65469

This photograph was taken from the top near the Market Place, with Castle Wynd up on the right. The street-name Millgate combines the Scandinavian word 'gata', or 'street', with its destination, the Castle Mill beside the Falls.

The Castle Keep 1908 59493

Looking up Millgate towards the same three-storey building that we see in 65469 (behind the horse and cart), on a day when the children were not at school. Just below the keep is the Corporation School, which had closed in 1902; it became a Territorial Army drill hall. Castle Walk would later acquire bollards to deter cars.

61

▶ *Millgate c1965* R32097

A similar view to 59493 shows an improved road surface, the aged persons' bungalows which replaced the Corporation School in about 1960, modern window-frames, and TV aerials. The double doors (left) lead into a yard where formerly there was a rope maker's walk.

▼ *Frenchgate 1913* 65464

This is Richmond's finest townscape: a steeply-curving cobbled street where handsome town houses mingle with small cottages. On the extreme right is Zetland House, next to the Ship Inn, and a few doors below is a butcher's shop, with slaughterhouse behind. The gas lamp near the children (left) marks Lombards Wynd. The pump (foreground) served Frenchgate Head.

▶ *The Green Howards War Memorial 1923* 74357

An area of poor cottages known as Frenchgate Head was squeezed onto this site. This war memorial was dedicated in 1921. The Green Howards (Alexandra, Princess of Wales's Own Yorkshire Regiment) were then based in the large barracks up nearby Gallowgate.

◄*Frenchgate c1955*
R32016

We are looking up from the Dundas Street junction. Few residents have cars. The terrace on the left replaced Bowes Hall, a medieval mansion, in 1787. Robert Willance lived in the whitewashed house with large chimneystack on the right (Willance miraculously survived when in 1606 his horse bolted and fell 200 feet). In the centre are two fine Georgian town houses, and St Agatha's, the High School for Girls until 1939.

*Lower Frenchgate
1929* 82547

This photograph looks
down towards the
Channel. Part of the tall
terrace on the right was
demolished to widen
Dundas Street. The
Grove, a fine Georgian
house built by Caleb
Readshaw, a wealthy
merchant of caps and
stockings knitted in
Swaledale, lies behind
the garden in the centre
of the picture.

The Channel 1929 82545

This street is so called because the Market Place, Frenchgate and Ryder's Wynd all drained into it. The coffee merchant
E W Coleman's van is parked outside his shop (centre); beside its window is an LNER train timetable - Station Road is off to
the left. Swale House on the extreme left was the home of Joe and Veronica Pease, great hosts of balls and parties.

St Nicholas 1924 75728

This is the oldest inhabited house in Richmond, founded in the 12th century as a medieval hospital (similar to an almshouse). From about 1900 the Hon Robert James created here a garden of historic importance, the prototype of Hidcote in Gloucestershire, and his second wife, Lady Serena, continued to live here and tend the garden until she died aged 99 in 2001.

The Convent 1898 41647

Now apartments, the convent was established c1850 by the Religious of the Assumption, who ran a girls' boarding school until 1993. Behind on the left is a house called Belle Vue, later Whitcliffe Grange, now demolished and replaced by council houses. Beyond is Westfields, one of the town's three medieval open fields.

RICHMOND ENVIRONS

THIS GROUP of photographs highlights historical trends such as the loss of shops, garages and other village facilities, victims of out-of-town supermarket shopping, and the disposal of traditional landed estates - of those included here, only Aske remains in hereditary ownership. The River Swale and its floods feature in this section too. In the churchyard at Marske there is a tombstone to two brothers, William and Joseph Rookby, who drowned aged 37 and 33 on 16 November 1771, an autumn day when, after heavy downpours, huge floods destroyed many bridges throughout the North of England.

The circuit begins west of Richmond north of the River Swale and swings round clockwise to an area west of Richmond south of the River Swale. We see Willance's Leap, about 2 miles west of the town centre but still within the Borough boundary, and quaint old villages, mostly older in origin than Richmond itself. The area south of the River Swale shows the considerable influence of Catterick Garrison.

WILLANCE'S LEAP
The Monuments and the Caravan Site c1965 R32080

We are looking west up Swaledale. Willance's Leap commemorates the miraculous deliverance from death of Robert Willance who, while hunting in 1606, was thrown over Whitcliffe Scar when a fog suddenly descended and disorientated his horse. The monuments mark the horse's final strides. Willance survived, minus one leg, until 1616, having recovered from his ordeal sufficiently well to serve as Alderman of Richmond in 1608.

MARSKE
General View
1913 65523

Marske is an attractive and unusual Swaledale village, neither nuclear nor linear, nestling in a fold of hills just above the River Swale. The tributary Marske Beck flows between the church and Marske Hall, and is crossed by Marske Bridge, a medieval ribbed structure.

MARSKE, *The Hall c1955* M378002

This was formerly the seat of the Hutton family, who produced two archbishops, both called Matthew, of York in 1595 and Canterbury in 1757. Marske Hall was rebuilt c1600 and Georgianised c1730, and behind it is a once-handsome stable block - the Huttons bred racehorses. The photograph shows some of the impressive trees which are a feature of Marske.

MARSKE
The Church 1913 65525

The ancient battlemented church of St Edmund King and Martyr has windows inscribed 'Iohn Hutton Sqvir 1683'. The interior, re-ordered by a later John Hutton c1830, contains his memorial with its fulsome epitaph, the Hutton family pew, and a Victorian royal coat of arms dated 1850.

► **MARSKE**
The Village
c1955 M378010

The Huttons were a capable family who made money, and spent much of it benevolently. Many local buildings bear testimony to their agricultural improvement. Just above the church are these pleasing stone houses; the one on the left was the erstwhile agent's house, and the one nearer the camera has a sundial over the door.

◄**KIRBY HILL**
The Church and the
Village 1913 65493a

The church of St Peter and St Felix serves the large parish of Kirkby Ravensworth. The tower is dated 1397. On the right, in the churchyard, is the former Grammar School, founded by the Rev John Dakyn in 1556, with a later headmaster's house. Across the village green the almshouse which he also endowed still stands.

▲ **ASKE HALL,** *The South Front 1893* 32283

This mansion just north of Richmond has been altered by successive owners: the Aske, Bowes and Wharton families, Sir Conyers D'Arcy, and, since 1763, the Dundas family, now ennobled as Marquesses of Zetland. The ivy was removed during a major restoration in the 1960s. The coats of arms relate to D'Arcy. The stable block to the right contains a 19th-century Italianate chapel.

◄ **ASKE HALL**
The West Front 1893 32284

Georgian additions on the left, since reduced in size, were designed by the York architect John Carr for Sir Lawrence Dundas. The garden has been redesigned at least twice since the photograph was taken, most recently by the present Marchioness of Zetland in 1994.

GILLING WEST
The Village 1913 65482

We are looking north, with the White Swan on the left and tall trees near the church in the centre. The grass in the foreground would soon bear a 1914-18 war memorial. The village shop and post office in the distance beyond the children still functions, but the shop-like Gilling Club (to the left of the woman in the middle of the road) has become a house.

► **GILLING WEST**
The Bridge c1950
G8301

This is a little-changed view; here, children play on bikes, and a cattle truck waits for its next load. Nearby there is still a village smithy. Just upstream of the old bridge crossing Gilling Beck, an elaborate Viking sword and carved stones were found in 1976. Gilling was an important Anglo-Saxon capital long before Richmond was founded.

◄ **GILLING WEST**
Hartforth Hall c1955
G8302

Hartforth Hall is now a hotel. Rainwater heads cast with the initials SC for Sheldon Cradock and the dates 1744 and 1792 suggest two phases of Georgian construction. The church-like tower was built for a water tank, and the clock commemorated the Cradock family's participation in the Boer War.

▲ **MIDDLETON TYAS,** *The Scotch Corner Hotel c1960* M73014

The hotel replaced the Three Tuns Inn in 1938, and was requisitioned by the army for residential and office use during the Second World War. This landmark, familiar to drivers on the A1, was in the 1950s THE place for film stars to stay on their way north, and most of the cars we see here are in the luxury class. Road improvements have left it just off the main road today.

◀**MIDDLETON TYAS**
The Shoulder of Mutton and the Post Office c1955 M73013

The pub remains, but the village shop and post office closed in March 2003. Soon afterwards a community group opened a village post office in the Memorial Hall, and also began raising funds and grants for adding a general shop with off-licence in 2004.

SKEEBY
The Village 1913
65490

This amazingly small-scale country lane is now not only surfaced and widened but installed with traffic-calming cushions to curb speed on the main Richmond-Darlington road. The building on the left became the village's Jubilee Hall in 1978.
The boy is carrying oars – most intriguing! Behind him is the small church of St Agatha.

EASBY
The Abbey with Richmond in the Distance 1898 41650

Just downstream of Richmond, Easby Abbey was founded about 1155 by the Premonstratensian or White Canons, an unenclosed order which worked in parishes. The building to the right partly behind the tree is the abbey gatehouse, once used as a stable for Georgian racehorses. It is pictured here with its roof on, but it is said that the owner took the roof off in order not to pay rates! The building behind the abbey ruins was the monastic corn watermill, where Thomas Park was still the miller in 1898.

EASBY, *The Abbey 1893* 32290

Little of the abbey church remains, but other buildings around the cloister are better preserved. This view shows the south transept (centre left), with the chapter house on the right. The ruined walls are now free of the lush vegetation shown here, and well consolidated, but Easby Abbey is still privately owned (although in English Heritage's guardianship).

EASBY
The Hall 1913 65503

The small hamlet of Easby still has fine trees and beautiful gardens. Easby House (or Hall) was built c1730, the road-facing side visible here in stone, but the back in the then more fashionable red brick so that it would show up in distant views. The Jaques family made alterations early in the 20th century. The service range (centre right) has been converted into cottages. Halfway down the lane to the left is the Echo Stone, on which children can stand and hear the echo from the Swale Valley when they call out 'Hello!'.

BROMPTON ON SWALE, *The Village 1913* 65494

We are looking east towards the Crown Inn (in the distance behind the walking man). A tarmac road surface and kerbed pavements are the main changes to this scene today. The stone cottages and red brick Methodist chapel have changed little except for some modern doors and windows.

CATTERICK
The Village 1913
65487

More trees obscure this view across the stream to Low Green, and Buckfast & Son's shop (behind the second tree from the right) has closed, but the buildings have changed little. St Anne's Church tower is visible behind the handsome Stepping Stones House. The stepping stones themselves look less serviceable now, but there is also a footbridge today.

▲ CATTERICK CAMP
Richmond Road 1953
C50020

Confusingly some distance away from Catterick village, Catterick Camp features particularly in the memories of many National Servicemen, perhaps including those outside the garage, decorated with crowns for the Coronation. The shops now tend to cater for less academic tastes than W H Smith (left), which in the 1950s was able to advertise itself as 'The Camp Bookshop'! Crasters was a men's outfitter.

▶ *detail from C50020*

▲ **HIPSWELL**
The Village 1913 66033

Was the smartly-dressed young lady (left) hoping to catch the eye of the young man with pony and trap? Although now absorbed into Catterick Garrison, Hipswell retains something of its village character with cottages around the green. A tradition that the 14th-century theologian John Wycliff was born in Hipswell in about 1324 is probably due to a mistake made by the Tudor historian John Leland.

◄ *detail from 66033*

HIPSWELL
The Church 1913
66032

St John's Church was built in 1811 to replace a chapel of ease of Catterick parish. The west belfry is particularly attractive. A timber screen inside came from the older building. In the churchyard are the distinctive war graves of servicemen from Catterick Camp, which lies between the villages of Hipswell, Scotton and Colburn.

HIPSWELL, *The Hall 1913* 66034

Hipswell Hall is a 15th-century fortified manor house built for the Fulthorpe family, whose coat of arms is carved on the bay window to the right. The estate passed to the Wandesfords of Kirklington, and over the front door is a plaque dated 1596 with the initials of George Wandesford. The lady by the gate would have no inkling of the military influx soon to come.

ARTHUR'S OVEN *1913* 65471

Billy Banks Wood, prominent in views from Castle Walk, is ancient 'hanging' woodland clinging to limestone rock on the south bank of the River Swale just west of Richmond Castle. This cave near Round Howe is known as Arthur's Oven; perhaps the name alludes to the legend that King Arthur and his Knights of the Round Table sleep in a vast cavern below the keep of Richmond Castle.

HUDSWELL BANK
Swaledale 1913 65516

We are looking west up
Swaledale from the hillside
below Hudswell; this scene
shows the classic V-shaped
profile of the river valley, so
typical of the Yorkshire
Dales. The fields of East
Underbanks Farm are
pastures and hay meadows
- the land is unsuitable for
arable crops. Willance's
Leap is on the scar to the
right.

DOWNHOLME
The Bridge 1913
65519

Masons' marks can be seen underneath the arches of this bridge, which was built in 1764 to connect Downholme with Marske. Damaged by the severe flood of 1771, two of the arches were rebuilt in 1773 at a cost of £1200; the contractors were Henry King and John Peacock.

DOWNHOLME, *The Church 1913* 65520

Inside the quaint little church of St Michael and All Angels is a George III coat of arms dated 1784, signed by the Richmond painter Robert Coatsworth; he helped to paint the scenery for the opening night of the Georgian Theatre Royal. Some distance away is the small village of Downholme, once bustling, with lead workings nearby, now close to Catterick Garrison's firing ranges.

INDEX

Arthur's Oven 85

Aske Hall 71

Brompton on Swale 79

Catterick 80-81

Catterick Camp 82

Downholme 88

Easby 78, 79

Gilling West 72-73, 74-75

Hipswell 83, 84, 85

Hudswell Bank 86-87

Kirby Hill 70

Marske 67, 68-69, 70-71

Middleton Tyas 75

Scotch Corner 75

Skeeby 76-77

Willance's Leap 14, 66

RICHMOND

Richmond 39, 44

    Bar 58, 59

Bridge 33, 34-35, 36, 37

Castle 22, 24-25, 28, 29, 30-31, 32-33, 34-35, 36, 37, 61

    Golden Tower 30

    Keep 29, 61

    Robin Hood's Tower 29

    Scolland's Hall 30-31

Castle Hill 55

Castle Walk 11, 31, 32

Catholic Church 54

Channel 64

Convent 65

Falls 38-39

Fleece Hotel 48

Frenchgate 62, 63, 64

Friars Wynd 49

Friary 46

Friary Gardens 48

Grammar School 43

Green 37

Green Howards War

    Memorial 63

Greyfriars Tower 47

Hospital 45

King Street 50-51, 52, 53

King's Head Hotel 25

Lower Frenchgate 64

Market Place 15, 16-17, 18-19, 20-21, 22-23, 24-25

Millgate 60, 61, 62

New Road 56-57

Newbiggin 55

Queens Road 13, 45

Railway Bridge 40

River Swale 40

St Mary's Church 41, 42

St Nicholas 65

Station Bridge 40

Tenace 39

Trinity Church 19, 22

NAMES OF SUBSCRIBERS

The following people have kindly supported this book by subscribing to copies before publication.

Alzheimers Society, Richmondshire

Andy & Sue Andrews, Richmond

Ron & Diane Applegarth, Richmond

Mr J C & Mrs Q V E Armitage & Family, Richmond

In memory of Fred & Edna Atkinson

Norma Merrington Atkinson

John Nigel James (Jack) Baldwin, Richmond

In memory of Amy E Bannaghan, Scotton

N Beetham, Richmond

Paul, Beryl, Nina Betteridge, Richmond

Steve & Maureen Bingham, Richmond

Josephine, Arthur & Steven Blackburn

In memory of Grandad John Bowers, Richmond

D Brambley & A Foster, Brompton-on-Swale

Pam, & Richard Brambley, Brompton-on-Swale

Tony & Carol Brend

Mr John Dennis Brigstock, Richmond

In memory of Eddie & Vi Brocklesby

Barbara Brookes, Richmond

Dennis Brown's Family, Brompton-on-Swale

Malcolm J Bryant, Richmond

Mr S R & Mrs H A Buckton, Richmond

The Callaghan Family, Richmond

Raymond Carter, Richmond

Bert & Doris Catt, Richmond, Yorkshire

Mrs A L Chefneux, Richmond

In memory of The Cherry Family, Richmond

Mrs J L Chisholm

The Clark Family, Richmond

Emma Clark, Richmond

F W Clark, Richmond

Mr & Mrs R Clark, Richmond

The Family Clarkson of Richmond

Dennys Newton Clarkson Esquire, Richmond

Christina Coates, Richmond

The Cook Family, Richmond

Naomi, Josephine & Mr M & Mrs C Cooper

Cradock Family, Days of Youth, Richmond

Cradock & Raggett of Richmond, Wed 2002

Barbara Crinson

Mrs Pat Croft, Richmond

Elsie Cundall

To my Dad, Trevor Davies, for all he's done

Ray Dea

The Deighton Family, Gilling West

John & Maura Deighton

Timothy J W Deighton

Bill & Ann Dickson, Richmond

Mr R D & Mrs G Dobinson, Richmond

Helen & Ronnie Dove, Germany

Dunkerley Family, Tasmania

Meana Eales

Derek Fay, Richmond

Mary & Alistair Ferguson, Richmond

Paul, Sandie & Alastair Fitton

The Forrest Family

In memory of John 'Jack' Foster, Richmond

In memory of Margot Fox, Richmond

Mr I R & Mrs J V Fraser

Martin French, Sweden

Gary & Kath, Oregon, USA, love Pam, Richmond

In memory of Gerald D Goldsbrough

William Denis & Margaret Grady, Richmond

Bill & Kate Green, Richmond

Mr A V Gutteridge & Mrs E Gutteridge

The Hallows Family, Richmond

Mr E P & Mrs G C Harker, Richmond

Mr C M Harrison, Richmond

To Peter Hatcher

In memory of Reg Hatcher

Paul & June Haxby, Richmond

J M Henderson

The Hindle Family, Catterick Garrison

In memory of my Father David Wm Hodgson

In memory of Stella & Alf Holbrook

David G Humphreys, Richmond

Mrs Joyce Hunt, a super Grandma
Mr & Mrs T S Hunt, Aulnay de Saintonge
To Maureen Hutchins, Richmond
Jane Jarvis
Laurie Jensen, Racine, WI, USA
Mr C F Johnson & Mrs E L Johnson
For our sons Josh & Adam, Richmond
Daniel James Kilvington-Mason, Richmond
Andy Kirby, Brompton-on-Swale
In memory of James 'Larry' Knight
In memory of Rita Lamb, Yorkshire
To Sonia Lawson, Richmond
In loving memory of Clive Lewis, Richmond
In loving memory of Len Lewis, Richmond
The Lloyd Family of Frenchgate, Richmond
F C & M J Lockwood
Jean & Don Ludlow, Richmond
Mr P M & Mrs M G Lumbard, Richmond
Patricia McColl & Matthew McColl
Mr S & Mrs A McCormack & Family, Richmond
Julie Martin
K R & M Morgan, Richmond
To my Mum on her birthday love Gemma xx
Salil Kumar Nag, Susmita Nag, Richmond
Mr & Mrs Nathan, Stanwick House, Richmond
Mary Dorothy O'Grady
Michael O'Grady
The Orton Family, Richmond
The Osborn Family, Richmond
In memory of Kenneth Partridge
Iris & David Peacock of Richmond, N Yorks
In memory of Greta & Anne-Marie Peirse
John F Place, Oxford
Mrs Janice & Mr Peter Plumb
Tiny & Christine Power, Richmond
Gordon & Jean Raine, Richmond
Les Reay
George W Richardson, Richmond
Dot & Gilbert Richmond, Richmond
Darryl Roberts, Richmond
In memory of Billy (Coco) & Freda Robinson
Mr & Mrs T Robinson, Richmond
Mr M I & Mrs P A Rookes, Richmond
Irene & Ian Rose, Richmond
In memory of George Russell, Richmond
To Peter Rutterford, In memory of David

Mr & Mrs J P Morrogh Ryan
The Ryde Family, Richmond
Victor Saggerson, Richmond
The Samways Family, Richmond
Dorothy Scott, Colburn, Richmond
The Scotting Family, Richmond
R Scotting
Anthony Francis Seline
Mrs Olive Severs, Richmond
Mr I M Sexton & Mrs I Sexton
N & K Sharpe, Richmond
Mr D W Shepherd, Richmond
Mr & Mrs D A Shout of Richmond, N Yorks
Mr A M & Mrs D P M Sillence, Richmond
With thanks to Angie Simpson, Richmond
David & Pat Simpson, Richmond
Richard D Smith
The Smiths Family, Richmond
Dennis Stedman of Richmond
Joseph H Stewart Jr, New Jersey, USA
G & L J Sunderland, Richmond
T R Sutton, Richmond
Dr Ian Swann
To Mr & Mrs B Tiller, Richmond
David & Carol Treweek
Mr A W R Tulip, Richmond
Mr L & Mrs J Verity, Brompton on Swale
Bruce & Elaine Ward, Brompton on Swale
Maj (Retd) David Ward Para TD LLB (hons)
David Ian Ward, Catterick Village
Michael Alan Ward, Richmond
In memory of Leslie Peter Wenham
Mr & Mrs P A N Whitesmith
Seamus Whittaker, Catterick Garrison
To Mark Whyman, Richmond
Maria Louise Wilde
Jean Lilian Wilkinson
Sandra Wilkinson
The Wood Family, Richmond 2002-2004
Mr & Mrs F L Wood
Mr P M Wood
Mr T L Wood
Ted & Margaret Wray, Richmond
In memory of Wrights, Frenchgate, Richmond
Stephen & Jane Yendall, Richmond

FRITH PRODUCTS & SERVICES

Francis Frith would doubtless be pleased to know that the pioneering publishing venture he started in 1860 still continues today. Over a hundred and forty years later, The Francis Frith Collection continues in the same innovative tradition and is now one of the foremost publishers of vintage photographs in the world. Some of the current activities include:

Interior Decoration

Today Frith's photographs can be seen framed and as giant wall murals in thousands of pubs, restaurants, hotels, banks, retail stores and other public buildings throughout the country. In every case they enhance the unique local atmosphere of the places they depict and provide reminders of gentler days in an increasingly busy and frenetic world.

Product Promotions

Frith products are used by many major companies to promote the sales of their own products or to reinforce their own history and heritage. Frith promotions have been used by Hovis bread, Courage beers, Scots Porage Oats, Colman's mustard, Cadbury's foods, Mellow Birds coffee, Dunhill pipe tobacco, Guinness, and Bulmer's Cider.

Genealogy and Family History

As the interest in family history and roots grows world-wide, more and more people are turning to Frith's photographs of Great Britain for images of the towns, villages and streets where their ancestors lived; and, of course, photographs of the churches and chapels where their ancestors were christened, married and buried are an essential part of every genealogy tree and family album.

Frith Products

All Frith photographs are available Framed or just as Mounted Prints and Posters (size 23 x 16 inches). These may be ordered from the address below. From time to time other products - Address Books, Calendars, Table Mats, etc - are available.

The Internet

Already fifty thousand Frith photographs can be viewed and purchased on the internet through the Frith websites and a myriad of partner sites.

For more detailed information on Frith companies and products, look at these sites:

www.francisfrith.co.uk
www.francisfrith.com
(for North American visitors)

See the complete list of Frith Books at:

www.francisfrith.co.uk

This web site is regularly updated with the latest list of publications from the Frith Book Company. If you wish to buy books relating to another part of the country that your local bookshop does not stock, you may purchase on-line.

For further information, trade, or author enquiries please contact us at the address below:
The Francis Frith Collection, Frith's Barn, Teffont, Salisbury, Wiltshire, England SP3 5QP.
Tel: +44 (0)1722 716 376 Fax: +44 (0)1722 716 881   Email: sales@francisfrith.co.uk

See Frith books on the internet at www.francisfrith.co.uk

FREE PRINT OF YOUR CHOICE

Mounted Print
Overall size 14 x 11 inches (355 x 280mm)

Choose any Frith photograph in this book.
Simply complete the Voucher opposite and
return it with your remittance for £2.25 (to cover
postage and handling) and we will print the
photograph of your choice in SEPIA (size 11 x 8
inches) and supply it in a cream mount with a
burgundy rule line (overall size 14 x 11 inches).
**Please note: photographs with a reference
number starting with a "Z" are not Frith
photographs and cannot be supplied under
this offer.**
Offer valid for delivery to UK addresses only.

**PLUS: Order additional Mounted Prints
at HALF PRICE - £7.49 each** (normally £14.99)
If you would like to order more Frith prints from
this book, possibly as gifts for friends and family,
you can buy them at half price (with no
additional postage and handling costs).

PLUS: Have your Mounted Prints framed
For an extra £14.95 per print you can have your
mounted print(s) framed in an elegant polished
wood and gilt moulding, overall size 16 x
13 inches (no additional postage and handling
required).

IMPORTANT!

**These special prices are only available if you use
this form to order . You must use the ORIGINAL
VOUCHER on this page (no copies permitted). We
can only despatch to one address. This offer
cannot be combined with any other offer.**

Send completed Voucher form to:
**The Francis Frith Collection, Frith's Barn,
Teffont, Salisbury, Wiltshire SP3 5QP**

CHOOSE A PHOTOGRAPH FROM THIS BOOK

Voucher for *FREE* and Reduced Price Frith Prints

*Please do not photocopy this voucher. Only the original is valid,
so please fill it in, cut it out and return it to us with your order.*

Picture ref no	Page no	Qty	Mounted @ £7.49	Framed + £14.95	Total Cost
		1	Free of charge*	£	£
			£7.49	£	£
			£7.49	£	£
			£7.49	£	£
			£7.49	£	£
			£7.49	£	£
Please allow 28 days for delivery			* Post & handling (UK)		£2.25
			Total Order Cost		£

Title of this book . . . .
I enclose a cheque/postal order for £ . . . .
made payable to 'The Francis Frith Collection'

OR please debit my Mastercard / Visa / Switch (Maestro)
/Amex card
(credit cards please on all overseas orders), details below

Card Number

Issue No (Switch only)   Valid from (Amex/Switch)

Expires   Signature

Name Mr/Mrs/Ms ....
Address ....
....
....
.... Postcode ....
Daytime Tel No ....
Email ....

Valid to 31/12/07

Would you like to find out more about Francis Frith?

We have recently recruited some entertaining speakers who are happy to visit local groups, clubs and societies to give an illustrated talk documenting Frith's travels and photographs. If you are a member of such a group and are interested in hosting a presentation, we would love to hear from you.

Our speakers bring with them a small selection of our local town and county books, together with sample prints. They are happy to take orders. A small proportion of the order value is donated to the group who have hosted the presentation. The talks are therefore an excellent way of fundraising for small groups and societies.

Can you help us with information about any of the Frith photographs in this book?

We are gradually compiling an historical record for each of the photographs in the Frith archive. It is always fascinating to find out the names of the people shown in the pictures, as well as insights into the shops, buildings and other features depicted.

If you recognize anyone in the photographs in this book, or if you have information not already included in the author's caption, do let us know. We would love to hear from you, and will try to publish it in future books or articles.

Our production team

Frith books are produced by a small dedicated team at offices in the converted Grade II listed 18th-century barn at Teffont near Salisbury, illustrated above. Most have worked with the Frith Collection for many years. All have in common one quality: they have a passion for the Frith Collection. The team is constantly expanding, but currently includes:

Paul Baron, Phillip Brennan, Jason Buck, John Buck, Ruth Butler, Heather Crisp, David Davies, Louis du Mont, Isobel Hall, Gareth Harris, Lucy Hart, Julian Hight, Peter Horne, James Kinnear, Karen Kinnear, Tina Leary, Stuart Login, David Marsh, Lesley-Ann Millard, Sue Molloy, Glenda Morgan, Wayne Morgan, Sarah Roberts, Kate Rotondetto, Dean Scource, Eliza Sackett, Terence Sackett, Sandra Sampson, Adrian Sanders, Sandra Sanger, Jan Scrivens, Julia Skinner, David Smith, Miles Smith, Lewis Taylor, Shelley Tolcher, Lorraine Tuck, Amanita Wainwright and Ricky Williams.